W9-ABQ-358

RACCOONS

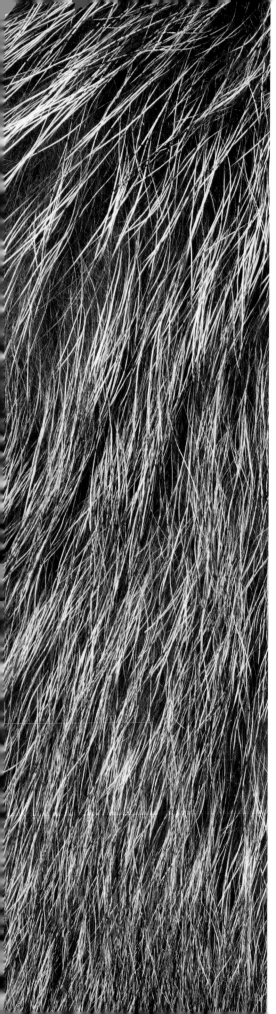

LIVING WILD

Published by Creative Education and Creative Paperbacks
P.O. Box 227, Mankato, Minnesota 56002
Creative Education and Creative Paperbacks are imprints of The Creative Company
www.thecreativecompany.us

Design and production by Mary Herrmann
Art direction by Rita Marshall
Printed in Malaysia

Photographs by Corbis (Blue Lantern Studio, DLILLC, Jasper Doest/Minden Pictures, Michael Durham/Visuals Unlimited, Tim Fitzharris/Minden Pictures, Scott Leslie/Minden Pictures, Arthur Morris, Rolf Nussbaumer/imagebroker, Kevin Schafer), Creative Commons Wikimedia (Bastique, Camazine, Monkeysdrawer, Ryskas), Dreamstime (Burdephotography, Goncharuk Maksym), Shutterstock (andamanec, Florian Andronache, Arteach1, B & T Media Group Inc., BMJ, Charles Brutlag, Gerald A. DeBoer, Leonid Dushin, Ella_K, Marlene Greene, jennyt, Heiko Kiera, Ivan Kuzmin, MarclSchauer, Martha Marks, olga_gl, rook76, Becky Sheridan, Pete Sherrard, David Spates, Michael J Thompson, Shane W Thompson, Mike Truchon, karl umbriaco, Krzysztof Wiktor)

Library of Congress Cataloging-in-Publication Data
Gish, Melissa.
Raccoons / Melissa Gish.
p. cm. — (Living wild)
Includes bibliographical references and index.
Summary: A look at raccoons, including their habitats, physical characteristics such as their facial masks, behaviors, relationships with humans, and their hunted status in the world today.
ISBN 978-1-60818-570-2 (hardcover)
ISBN 978-1-62832-171-5 (pbk)
1. Raccoon—Juvenile literature. I. Title.

QL737.C26G55 2015
599.76'32—dc23   2014028012

CCSS: RI.5.1, 2, 3, 8; RST.6-8.1, 2, 5, 6, 8; RH.6-8.3, 4, 5, 6, 7, 8

First Edition HC 9 8 7 6 5 4 3 2 1
First Edition PBK 9 8 7 6 5 4 3 2 1

CREATIVE EDUCATION • CREATIVE PAPERBACKS

RACCOONS

Melissa Gish

It's nearly midnight, and a full moon shines
over the Florida Everglades. A raccoon

ambles through the underbrush toward a
muddy mound at the water's edge.

It's nearly midnight, and a full moon shines over the Florida Everglades. A raccoon ambles through the underbrush toward a muddy mound at the water's edge. It has smelled something edible buried beneath the sand and leaves. Its nimble hands soon uncover a treasure: American crocodile eggs. The raccoon tears into the leathery eggs with its sharp claws, scooping out the juicy contents. Suddenly, a crocodile bursts from the water and races up the bank to defend her nest. Screeching, the raccoon drops its meal and lurches backward, tumbling down the mound. The crocodile lunges forward as the raccoon runs for the nearest tree. Up it climbs. The crocodile grunts and hisses at the intruder. From the safety of the branches, the raccoon watches the crocodile return to the nest and cover the surviving eggs. Tomorrow night, the raccoon will try again.

WHERE IN THE WORLD THEY LIVE

■ **Common Raccoon**
North America

■ **Pygmy Raccoon**
Mexico's Cozumel
Island

■ **Crab-eating
Raccoon**
Central and South
America

Native to the Western Hemisphere, the three species of
raccoon include the island-dwelling endangered pygmy
raccoon, the tropical crab-eating raccoon, and the
increasingly urban North American (or common) raccoon,
which has also been introduced to Europe and Asia. The
colored squares represent some of the areas in which
raccoons are found today.

HANDY CRITTERS

The critically endangered Cozumel Island coati (pictured) is often mistaken for its relative, the Cozumel Island raccoon.

hree species and several subspecies of raccoons help make up the family Procyonidae (*PRO-sy-ON-ih-die*), named for a Greek phrase meaning "before the dog." All are **endemic** to the Americas. The North American, or common, raccoon is widespread from Canada to Argentina and can be successful in a variety of habitats, from remote forests to bustling cities. But some other raccoons are rare and even endangered. While the crab-eating raccoon of Central and South America enjoys a stable population, Mexico's pygmy raccoon is in trouble. In 2008, this raccoon, also called the Cozumel Island raccoon, was upgraded on the International Union for Conservation of Nature (IUCN) Red List of Threatened Species from endangered to critically endangered. An estimated 250 to 300 pygmy raccoons remain on the planet.

In addition, more than 25 subspecies of the common raccoon have been confirmed, including 4 island subspecies. About 2,000 Bahaman raccoons inhabit New Providence Island in the Bahamas, while roughly the same number of Guadeloupe raccoons is found on

Raccoons can withstand a drop of 35 feet (10.7 m), usually without injury, and squeeze into any space big enough for their head.

Basse-Terre and Grande-Terre islands in the Lesser Antilles. The Tres Marias raccoon once made its home on the three largest islands of Mexico's Islas Marías. Now it survives only on Isla María Madre and is thought to number fewer than 200. In 1996, the IUCN categorized these three raccoon subspecies as endangered. The fourth island subspecies, the Barbados raccoon, was last seen on the island of Barbados in 1964 and is now considered **extinct**.

Of all small **mammals**, raccoons have the greatest size variation among individuals. Some can reach lengths of 15 to 30 inches (38.1–76.2 cm) from nose to rear, not counting the tail, which can add up to 16 inches (40.6 cm). A raccoon's weight depends entirely on its environment and available diet. Raccoons typically weigh the most in fall, after they have built up their fat reserves for the coming winter. Common raccoons tend to average 8 to 20 pounds (3.6–9.1 kg), but the largest wild raccoon ever recorded in the United States was found in Wisconsin. It weighed more than 62 pounds (28.1 kg). The *Guinness Book of World Records* listed a pet raccoon named Bandit as the world's heaviest raccoon.

To break up their scent trail, raccoons may climb trees, jumping from one to another before returning to the ground.

Common raccoons found in places such as Florida's Sanibel Island are not considered island raccoons.

At the time of his death in 2004, Bandit weighed nearly 75 pounds (34 kg)! On the other end of the scale, raccoons in the Florida Keys, which have little more to eat than shellfish plucked from marshes, typically weigh about four pounds (1.8 kg).

A raccoon's coat, called pelage, varies in color from reddish to gray or black. Raccoons have two layers of fur to keep them warm. About 90 percent of their coat is made up of short, wavy underfur that grows to about an inch (2.5 cm) long. The rest of the pelage is made up of long, coarse guard hairs. These hairs are hollow and can trap warm air to provide the raccoon with **insulation** from the cold during winter. Raccoons in cold climates develop pelage that grows denser and longer throughout the winter before it is shed in spring. Raccoons that live in warm climates have thinner coats year round.

Perhaps the raccoon's most striking—yet mysterious— feature is its black facial mask. Because raccoons are nocturnal, or active at night, some scientists suggest that the markings around the eyes may serve to enhance night vision. Since the color black absorbs light, more available light could be drawn toward the eyes. Others suggest that

Raccoons are easily distinguished from other animals by their characteristic facial markings.

A raccoon's whiskers, which normally lie flat against its face, stick out when the animal is curious or alarmed.

the black fur, similar to eye black worn by football players and other athletes, cuts the sun's glare while raccoons forage around water. Still others believe the mask might aid in defense, making the raccoon's eyes look bigger and more fearsome to enemies. Another distinctive marking on a raccoon's fur is its ringed tail. Five to seven dark rings alternate with the raccoon's lighter fur the entire length of the tail. Raccoons use their tail for balance while climbing and also for support while sitting upright.

Raccoons can eat a variety of food, from birds, snakes, and eggs to kitchen scraps pilfered from urban trash cans. The raccoon's hand-like front paws enable this animal to make a meal of just about anything. Soft, hairless, black skin covers the underside of the paws. Unlike most mammals, raccoons have no fleshy webbing between the five digits on each paw. The front digits are long and finger-like, with one functioning similar to a thumb. This paw structure allows the raccoon to hold and manipulate objects in ways that most other small animals cannot. Such **dexterity** means that raccoons can unhook latches, turn doorknobs, and pull lids off containers. Raccoons also demonstrate a skill called

A raccoon's ringed tail can account for more than half of the animal's total body length.

tactile discrimination, which is the ability to understand details about an object based on touch alone. Raccoons can reach into tight spaces to work objects free, and they can feel their way through mud to locate buried food. Raccoons also scratch and clean their food of debris before eating it, a behavior called dousing. This action is likely what gave the raccoon its name, which originated as the Algonquian word "aroughcun" (*uh-ruh-COON*) that British explorer Captain John Smith misspelled in his 1612 journal. The original word, *arahkunem* or *arahkun*, spoken to Smith by the Powhatan Indians, means "he scratches with the hands."

Raccoons are clever hunters and foragers equipped with keen senses. The raccoon's eyes have a reflective layer of tissue called a tapetum lucidum. This tissue collects light and concentrates it in the center of the **retina**, allowing the raccoon to see well in low light. The tissue also causes eyeshine, making the eyes reflect color when a light is shined on them. The raccoon's eyeshine varies from yellow to green in color. Raccoons have an acute sense of smell and a highly receptive nose. Neurons, or sensitive cells, in the moist surface around the nostrils, called the rhinarium, can detect food beneath two inches (5.1 cm) of sand or soil. Raccoons' powerful jaws contain two pairs of sharp upper and lower canine teeth and six pairs of pointed incisors at the front of the mouth, which are used for ripping meat. Twelve pairs of grinding teeth along the sides of the jaw can pulverize vegetation, nuts, and even small bones.

Many wildlife biologists can identify animals, even in total darkness, by the color of their eyeshine.

Studies indicate that, once a raccoon solves a problem, it can remember the solution for as long as three years.

Ringtails are agile climbers whose long tails help them flip cartwheels to make sudden changes in direction.

RAMBUNCTIOUS RACCOONS

O ther members of Procyonidae share some of the raccoon's physical characteristics. However, they have varied habitats and diets. In South America, coatis live on the ground and eat rodents, tarantulas, and fallen fruit. Neighboring kinkajous live in trees and eat leaves, herbs, and ripe fruit. Raccoons' closest relatives, the ringtails, live in the rocky deserts of Mexico and the American Southwest, catching snakes and lizards in winter and munching berries in summer. The common raccoon has **adapted** to North American winters and to an omnivorous diet, which means it eats both animals and plants. Such flexibility has allowed raccoons to thrive as easily in cities and suburbs as they do in forests and on farms.

The raccoon is one of the most widely distributed animals in North America. It prefers forested habitats near a water source, such as a stream or marsh. Raccoons live in a particular area, called a home range, that is usually within half a mile (0.8 km) of a water source. The size of a home range depends on the amount of food available. In a marsh, for example, where fish, frogs, eggs,

Kinkajous are strictly nocturnal, safely sleeping the days away in hollow trees or high up in shady nests.

invertebrates, and vegetation are abundant, a home range might be the size of three football fields. But in sparsely forested foothills, where food is scarce, a home range might be the size of 1,000 football fields. Up to 4 males may share a home range separate from female groups, which can number up to 12. Raccoons rotate dens, rarely sleeping in the same place more than two days in a row. Hollow spaces inside tree trunks or branches are preferred den sites. When trees are not available, raccoons may hide inside man-made structures—barns, sheds, and even attics. Raccoons will sometimes use burrows dug out by other animals such as badgers or woodchucks if the burrow shows signs of abandonment.

Raccoons do not defend their home ranges against other raccoons unless food is scarce. Home ranges typically overlap, and raccoons cross paths on a regular basis. Scientists once thought raccoons lived alone, but research conducted in the early 2000s revealed that raccoons engage in several different social behaviors that change seasonally. For about four months out of the year, females isolate themselves from other raccoons to give birth and raise their babies, called kits. The rest of the time, they live with other females and their offspring, sleeping together and, if food is abundant, eating together. Family groups composed of a female and two generations of both male and female offspring are also common. A group of raccoons is called a gaze, referring to their dark, piercing eyes. Males gather in groups of three or four for specific purposes: During cold weather, they sleep together; if there is enough food to go around, they share; and during mating season, a band of males will chase away invaders competing for females. Mature males, called boars, and mature females, called sows, come together only once or twice a year for a period

A raccoon might make its den in such places as a hollow log, an abandoned burrow, a cave, or a tree.

Though kits constantly chirp and chatter to stay in contact with their mother, adults vocalize much less.

of three or four days to mate. Beyond that, they tend to avoid each other.

Both boars and sows reach maturity by the age of one. Males are attracted to females by their scent. Depending on where a raccoon lives, mating takes place between January and June. Females are able to get pregnant only a few days out of the year. Fifty-four to 70 days after successful mating, between 2 and 5 kits are born. Before she gives birth, the sow selects a protected place, such as a tall tree, where she and her offspring will be safest from predators. Born blind and deaf, the kits are about four inches (10.2 cm) long and weigh less than three ounces (85 g). Despite having lighter fur than their mother, kits are born with a visible face mask. They immediately begin feeding on the milk produced by their mother.

It takes about three weeks for the kits' ear canals to open so that they can hear. Their eyes open a few days later. The kits remain hidden in the den for another six to eight weeks. Now, at 10 times their birth weight, the kits are allowed to explore the world and eat solid food that their mother teaches them to find. At this time, the sow moves her kits to a ground den. Scientists have suggested

When mother raccoons are killed or trapped and relocated, it is unlikely that their orphaned kits will survive.

Raccoons can forage in water as cold as 50 °F (10 °C) for hours without losing their sense of touch.

this action prevents the rambunctious youngsters from being killed by falling from the tree den. When they are about four months old, the young raccoons are fully **weaned**. Their mother teaches them how to hunt, forage, make a den, and avoid predators. The young disperse and establish their own home ranges when they are about 14 months old. Females typically stay close to their mothers, but males can travel up to 12 miles (19.3 km) away from their birthplace, where they will find unrelated females with which to mate the following spring. Only about half of all raccoon kits will survive their first year.

Young raccoons are vulnerable to starvation in cold weather. If they remain with their mother, she can help them find food, but many raccoons lose their mothers and are left alone. Finding sufficient food, especially through snow cover, is too great a challenge for many young raccoons. A variety of predators, from coyotes and bobcats to great horned owls, regularly prey on young raccoons. But humans are the leading cause of raccoon deaths. Adult raccoons are hunted extensively for their fur, and many are hit by vehicles on roadways. The second leading cause of death in raccoons is disease. One particularly devastating disease is distemper, a virus that first affects the respiratory system and eventually leads to brain damage. Infected raccoons and other animals in close contact with each other can spread the infection. Raccoons are also susceptible to rabies, which is a virus that affects the central nervous system. An infected animal can spread the disease to other animals and even humans through bites that pierce the skin. In the wild, raccoons rarely survive more than three or four years. However, in captivity, raccoons have been known to live for 20 years.

Bobcats generally hunt rabbits and hares, but they also prey on young raccoons, if they have the opportunity.

Like other woodland creatures, raccoons have been featured in folklore, fairy tales, and storybooks for centuries.

MAGIC AND MISCHIEF

R accoons have been given many names in American Indian and First Nations traditions, most of which refer to the same distinctive behaviors or markings. The Seminole name for raccoon was *wood-ko*, meaning "one who rubs," while the Mohican name was *sha-we*, meaning "one who grasps." The Mandan name *nashi* meant "one with blackened face and feet," and the Hopi name *shiuaa* meant "painted one." Some **cultures** believed the raccoon had connections to the spirit world. The Huron-Iroquois called the raccoon *gahado-goka-gogosa*, or "masked demon spirit," and the Cheyenne named it *macho-on*, or "one who makes magic." The Aztecs of ancient Mexico had several names for the crab-eating raccoon. Males were *mapachitli*, or "one who takes everything in his hands"; females were *see-oh-at-la-ma-kas-kay*, or "she who talks with gods"; and kits were *ee-yah-mah-tohn*, or "little old ones who know things."

Because raccoons are inquisitive animals, they have traditionally been associated with mischief and trickery. In the folklore of many native peoples of North America, raccoons are clever creatures typically up to no good, and

An island raccoon was part of a series of 2007 French stamps commemorating endangered animals in foreign lands.

Raccoons are mostly absent from Arizona, Nevada, and Utah, where water and vegetation are too scarce.

Often featuring earflaps, most modern raccoon hats are made with fur and moisture-resistant fabric.

Raccoons were introduced to Alaska in the 1930s for the fur trade and have become pests in many southern Alaska cities.

their rivalry with other animals is at the center of many tales. Their distinctive markings and human-like hands make raccoons the focus of many pourquoi, or stories that explain how things came to be.

A story from the Ojibwa tradition tells how the raccoon went to the crayfish and told them that he had discovered a wonderful muddy lake—just the kind crayfish love—on the other side of a hill. The raccoon offered to give them a ride, so they climbed onto his back. Off they went over the hill, but the crayfish did not make it to the lake. Instead, the raccoon had a hearty meal in the shade of a tree.

A story from the Biloxi Indians of the Gulf Coast region suggests why raccoons and opossums are nocturnal. One morning, the raccoon went to his favorite crayfish pond. He found footprints in the mud and all the crayfish hiding. Then he went to his favorite persimmon tree and discovered all the ripe fruit had been taken. He saw opossum footprints close by. So he decided to get up even earlier the next morning to beat the opossum to the pond and the persimmons. His plan worked, but the day after that, the raccoon found that the opossum had beaten

Areas of standing water are attractive to playful raccoons but are also dangerous for spreading disease.

him there once again. The two went back and forth for some time, each getting up earlier, until finally, neither the opossum nor the raccoon slept at all during the night. Instead, they raced each other all night to be the first to the crayfish pond and the persimmon tree.

Pourquoi tales about the raccoon's distinctive markings are abundant in folklore. A story from the Nez Perce blames it on a tussle between Raccoon and Coyote. One day, the story goes, Coyote was napping by the river's edge. He had just cooked and eaten a salmon over an open fire. Raccoon sneaked up on Coyote and gently moved his rival's paws into the embers. The hot coals

X. FATTY COON AND THE MONSTER

One night Fatty Coon was strolling along the road that wound through the valley. He was in no hurry, for he had just left Farmer Green's apple orchard, where he had bolted all the apples he could possibly eat. The night was dark and though it was not very late, all the country people seemed to be in bed. There were no farmers driving along the road. Fatty had it all to himself. And so he walked slowly homewards. It was then that the terrible monster almost caught him.

This is how it all happened. There was a br-br-br-r-r-r in the air. Fatty really should have heard it long before he did. But he had eaten so many apples that he had begun to feel sleepy; and his ears were not so sharp as they should have been. And when at last Fatty heard that br-r-r-r it was quite loud. He was startled. And he stopped right in the middle of the road to listen. Fatty had never heard such a sound before.

The strange animal was on him before he knew it. Its glaring eyes blinded him. And if it had not screamed at him Fatty would never have escaped. It was the terrible screech of the monster which finally made Fatty jump. It was a frightful cry—like six wildcats all wailing together. And Fatty leaped to one side of the road just before the monster reached him.

from Sleepy-Time Tales: The Tale of Fatty Coon, *by Arthur Scott Bailey (1877–1949)*

jolted Coyote awake, and before Raccoon could escape, Coyote grabbed Raccoon by the ears and dragged him through the embers, smudging black all over his hands and feet. Then he smacked Raccoon in the face. Raccoon tried to get away, but Coyote grabbed him by the tail. When Raccoon finally freed himself, he was left with black on his hands, feet, ears, face, and tail.

In the 18th century, American settlers learned from the **indigenous** peoples that raccoons in full winter pelage had some of the warmest fur to be found. Raccoons were trapped, and their **pelts** became a valuable material for hats and coats. Fur hats called coonskin caps included the raccoon's tail hanging down in the back. Benjamin Franklin famously wore a coonskin cap on a 1776 trip to France, and explorer Meriwether Lewis sported one during the Lewis and Clark Expedition of 1804–06. Songs and images of frontiersmen Davy Crockett and Daniel Boone (who never really wore coonskin caps) fueled the public's demand for these hats. Interest in raccoon pelts switched from hats to men's coats in the 1920s, a fad that lasted less than a decade. Then, in the 1950s, Walt Disney produced a series of television shows

Raccoons do not hibernate, but they do sleep in a den for several weeks without eating—a period called winter rest.

Raccoon kits are highly playful, which helps them learn about the world and test their survival abilities.

and movies about Davy Crockett and Daniel Boone. The popularity of Disney's characters temporarily reignited a love for the coonskin cap, and children across America wanted one, at an average cost of $1.98. Coonskin caps are still sold through fur retailers, generally for their warmth, but today, they cost around $100.

In 1969, Walt Disney produced a film version of Sterling North's 1963 book *Rascal*, the true story of one year in the author's childhood when he raised a pet raccoon. Rascal became a loving companion to the young Sterling but ultimately needed to live free. The book and movie were hugely popular in Japan, where a 52-episode television series was created in 1977. The series, called *Rascal the Raccoon*, led to the importation of thousands of raccoons to Japan to be sold as pets. Today, the descendants of those pets have taken to living in wilderness areas throughout the island nation. Another Disney raccoon was Meeko, a character in the 1995 animated movie *Pocahontas* and its 1998 sequel *Pocahontas II: Journey to a New World*. Meeko is clever and greedy, stealing food every chance he gets.

Walt Disney Studios was also responsible for

the release of *Guardians of the Galaxy*, a 2014 three–dimensional movie featuring the superhero team first introduced by Marvel Comics in 1969 and relaunched in 2008. Expert marksman Rocket Raccoon is a major character in the comic books and film. He is also a playable character in the video games *Ultimate Marvel vs. Capcom 3* and *Lego Marvel Superheroes*. Perhaps one of the most enduring raccoon characters in popular culture is Ranger Rick, a National Wildlife Federation (NWF) mascot and namesake of a children's nature magazine since 1967. Ranger Rick also has a page filled with games, articles, and videos on the NWF website.

Books, comics, and magazines have long depicted Daniel Boone wearing his signature coonskin cap.

The raccoon ancestor Chapalmalania, *which went extinct 1.8 million years ago, was first thought to be a bear.*

BUILDING A SMARTER RACCOON

Fossil remains dating to about 30 million years ago once placed raccoons in the Mustelidae, or weasel, family. However, fossils of the first direct ancestors of raccoons, coatis, and other procyonids were found in France and Germany throughout the 1900s, offering proof that raccoons had separated from weasels at least 20 million years ago. Since North America and Asia were connected by land at that time in Earth's history, these small animals spread from Europe to Asia and then through the Americas.

Over millions of years, the prehistoric procyonids in Europe and Asia died out, but the ones in South America survived drastic climate and habitat changes. Up until about 10 million years ago, procyonids were squirrel-sized creatures that lived underground in burrows. As predators increased in size and number, the procyonids adapted to living in trees, where they were safer. They changed their eating habits from digging for worms and grubs to seeking out fruit, nuts, bird eggs, and tree-dwelling insects and lizards. Kinkajous and other tree-dwelling procyonids split off from those that returned to

Raccoons have a bite force of roughly 53 pounds per square inch (3.7 kg/sq cm)—about the same as a domestic cat's.

Because raccoons move with a bearish lumber, scientists first classified them as part of the bear family.

Raccoons can run up to 15 miles (24.1 km) per hour, as demonstrated by urban raccoons racing across busy streets and highways.

the ground and became coatis, ringtails, and crab-eating raccoons. Some procyonids then moved northward, and by about 2.5 million years ago, they had **evolved** into the raccoons that we know today.

Because some raccoons exist in small habitats restricted to islands, they have gradually become somewhat smaller than raccoons on the North American continent. This process is called insular dwarfism, and it causes animals to conserve resources. However, even though island raccoons are at the top of their **food chains**, they cannot compete with humans. Habitat destruction for the expansion of tourist areas is driving island raccoons toward extinction, particularly on Cozumel. Tourism there emerged in the 1970s and has been growing steadily ever since. Cozumel is about six times smaller than the state of Rhode Island, and the pygmy raccoon exists only in one small wetland area on the island's northwest corner. Since 1994, research on Cozumel has been conducted and conservation efforts have been recommended by a team of scientists led by Dr. Alfredo D. Cuarón of the National Institute of Ecology and Climate Change in Mexico. Without serious conservation efforts, the team reported, pygmy raccoons will surely

disappear. Despite their endangered status, neither the pygmy nor any of the island raccoon subspecies receives legal protection from hunting or trapping. In addition, the introduction of pets to the islands in recent decades has had a devastating effect on the survival rate of raccoon kits, which are often attacked by dogs and cats. And an increasing population of stray dogs and cats has led to the spread of disease and **parasites** that threaten island raccoons.

Elsewhere in the world, raccoons are abundant, for their populations have not suffered permanently despite human influence. Raccoons are legally hunted and

The pygmy raccoon forages for shellfish that live in mangrove swamps and sandy wetland areas.

Raccoons are known for their messy nighttime antics of scavenging in people's garbage cans.

trapped in most of the U.S. and in Canada. Their fur is useful, and their meat, similar to dark-meat chicken, is edible. While raccoons in spacious wilderness and rural areas tend to shy away from people, raccoons in urban settings have lost their fear of humans. Dr. Stan Gehrt, a professor of wildlife ecology at Ohio State University, is the foremost authority on raccoon **physiology** and behavior. Among the discoveries Gehrt has made since 1984 is a startling fact about urban raccoons: they not only grow fatter, reproduce more, and live longer than their country cousins, but they also may be evolving into smarter animals. As generations of raccoons grow up in cities, they have learned where and when the best trash is available to eat, where they should and should not hide during the day, and how best to avoid the perils of predators and cars—two dangers that typically take rural raccoons by surprise. It is the raccoon's adaptability as a species, Gehrt says, that has allowed this animal to thrive while living side-by-side with humans.

A study performed by Dr. Suzanne MacDonald and Dr. Marc Dupuis-Desormeaux, two biologists at York University in Toronto, was the subject of the 2012 PBS documentary *Raccoon Nation*. For the study, raccoons in three different parts of Toronto were captured in wire traps using cat food as bait and then tranquilized to make them fall asleep. A collar holding a mini computer hard drive and a radio transmitter was placed around each raccoon's neck. The collars collected data on the raccoons' movements and also sent a signal every 5 to 15 minutes so that MacDonald could plot their locations on a map. This was the first study of

The use of live traps is an easy and humane method of capturing raccoons for research or relocation.

On a junk-food diet, urban raccoons suffer from more tooth decay and obesity than rural or wilderness area raccoons.

Though glass and sheet metal are too smooth for them to grip, raccoons can climb nearly any other surface.

Although the practice is discouraged, some people raise raccoons as pets and reintroduce them to the wild.

its kind, prompting other researchers to model future investigations after it as attempts are made to guide raccoon management plans.

One serious management issue confronting both rural and urban raccoons is rabies. Of all North American mammals, raccoons have the highest rate of rabies infection. While domestic animals can be **vaccinated** against rabies infection, humans who are bitten by rabid animals must undergo treatment by injections to prevent illness. In some parts of the U.S. and Canada, residents are encouraged to set out food containing a vaccine that will prevent rabies in raccoons. Elsewhere, animal control professionals must put down rabid raccoons to avoid spreading the disease to other animals or people.

Some scientists believe that because raccoons are highly curious, they may actually welcome the challenges posed by obstacles put in their path, such as barricades on buildings and latches on trash containers. The problem-solving skills needed to get around such barriers may be leading to growing intelligence in raccoons. As raccoons adapt to life among humans, researchers suggest, they develop strategies for avoiding us.

Dr. Gehrt believes we can never learn all there is to know about raccoons because their behaviors are constantly changing. "The more we've looked at raccoons," Dr. Gehrt said, "the harder they are to understand." Island-dwelling raccoons may never get the chance to adapt to urban life, but mainland raccoons are already learning how to share a changing world with humans. Now it is up to us to find ways of sharing the world with ever-adaptable raccoons.

When people feed wild raccoons, it encourages the animals to take up residence in and around human dwellings.

ANIMAL TALE: RACCOON PAYS FOR HIS TRICKERY

Raccoons appear in the legends of virtually every North American Indian tribe. They typically play the role of a trickster. In this story from the Lakota people of the North American Great Plains, Raccoon pays a price for his deception of Crayfish.

Crayfish looks fierce with his sharp, powerful claws, but he is a timid creature. He eats only dead things. Raccoon eats just about anything he can get his paws on, but he especially loves to eat crayfish.

One day, Crayfish was roaming along the riverbank looking for food. Raccoon thought he would play a trick on Crayfish. He sprawled out on his back and held his breath. He remained very still as Crayfish approached.

"Are you dead?" Crayfish asked. Raccoon did not answer. Crayfish cautiously pinched Raccoon's nose. There was no reaction. Then, Crayfish pinched Raccoon's soft paw. There was no movement. Next, Crayfish pinched Raccoon's tail. Still nothing. "You must be dead," Crayfish said. "I will go tell the village so that everyone can feast on dead Raccoon." And Crayfish hurried away.

After Crayfish was long gone, Raccoon leaped to his feet and burst out laughing. "What a fool," Raccoon said. "We'll see who eats whom."

Blue Jay had been watching the entire scene from a tree branch above the riverbank. "You're going to be sorry," he warned. "No good can possibly come from such a deceitful trick."

"Mind your own business," Raccoon retorted, positioning himself back on the riverbank.

Crayfish returned with all his kin. They found Raccoon right where Crayfish had left him—and he appeared to be quite dead.

"Are you sure he's dead?" Crayfish's sister asked, pinching Raccoon's nose. There was no reaction.

"Perhaps he's faking," said Crayfish's friend, pinching Raccoon's soft paw. There was no movement.

"We should make sure," said Crayfish's brother, pinching Raccoon's tail. Nothing. "He's dead, all right!"

All the crayfish were excited to have such a feast before them. They danced and sang. They climbed all over Raccoon, waving their claws. The whole time, Raccoon bit his lip to keep from laughing.

Next, Crayfish and his brothers hurried off to the forest to gather sticks for a fire. Crayfish's sisters dug a pit in the ground. Raccoon, tired of his game, fell asleep.

Several hours passed. Raccoon awoke and found himself trapped in a deep pit with a fire burning over him.

He scrambled out of the pit and found the crayfish still celebrating. "He's alive!" Crayfish cried out. "Run!" And all the crayfish disappeared into the river.

When Raccoon rubbed his paws against his itchy eyes, he noticed they were covered in black soot. He ran to the river's edge to wash his paws, but the black would not come off. He looked at his reflection in the water and leaped back in horror. "What have they done to me?" he cried. His tail was stained, and black soot ringed his eyes where he had rubbed his paws on them.

From his perch in a tree, Blue Jay laughed. "I warned you that your deception would come to no good. Now you will bear the marks of your sneaky trick for all your days to come."

GLOSSARY

adapted – changed to improve its chances of survival in its environment

cultures – particular groups in a society that share behaviors and characteristics that are accepted as normal by that group

dexterity – skill or agility in using the hands or body to perform tasks

endemic – native to and confined to a certain geographical location

evolved – gradually developed into a new form

extinct – having no living members

food chains – systems in nature in which living things are dependent on each other for food

hibernate – to spend the winter in a sleep-like state in which breathing and heart rate slow down

indigenous – originating in a particular region or country

insulation – the state of being protected from the loss of heat

invertebrates – animals that lack a backbone, including shellfish, insects, and worms

mammals – warm-blooded animals that have a backbone and hair or fur, give birth to live young, and produce milk to feed their young

parasites – animals or plants that live on or inside another living thing (called a host) while giving nothing back to the host; some parasites cause disease or even death

pelts – the skins of animals with the fur or wool still attached

physiology – the scientific study of the functions and parts of living organisms' bodies

retina – a layer or lining in the back of the eye that is sensitive to light

vaccinated – given a substance to provide protection from a disease

weaned – made the young of a mammal accept food other than nursing milk

SELECTED BIBLIOGRAPHY

Fleming, Susan. *Nature: Raccoon Nation*. DVD. Toronto: Optix Digital Pictures, 2012.

Lopez, Andrea Dawn. *When Raccoons Fall through Your Ceiling: The Handbook for Coexisting with Wildlife*. Denton, Tex.: University of North Texas Press, 2002.

National Geographic Kids. "Animals: Raccoon." http://kids.nationalgeographic.com/content/kids/en_US/animals/raccoon/.

New Hampshire Public Television. "NatureWorks: Raccoon." http://www.nhptv.org/natureworks/raccoon.htm.

Yery, Erika. "Rescue Report: Raccoons—Facts and Fancies." Wildlife Rescue League. http://www.wildliferescueleague.org/pdf/raccoon.pdf.

Zeveloff, Samuel I. *Raccoons: A Natural History*. Washington, D.C.: Smithsonian Institution, 2002.

Note: Every effort has been made to ensure that any websites listed above were active at the time of publication. However, because of the nature of the Internet, it is impossible to guarantee that these sites will remain active indefinitely or that their contents will not be altered.

The ability of raccoons to adapt to their changing environments makes them some of Earth's most successful animals.

INDEX